Copyright: @Wooden House Books, 2024

Catherine Stephenson
Illustrated by Hiruni Kariyawasam
ISBN: 978-1-7390914-3-9

All rights reserved. This book or any portion thereof may not be reproduced or used in any manner whatsoever without the express written permission of the publisher, except for the use of brief quotations in a book review.

First Printing, 2024
Wooden House Books
www.woodenhousebooks.com

Catherine Stephenson. Illustrated by Hiruni Kariyawasam.

The Kids' Book of

FAMILY
CHANGES

Understanding Divorce and Separation and Managing Feelings

A kid's guide to changes at home.

When parents decide not to live together any more, it can feel like a big change for children.

If this is happening in your family, you might feel sad, worried, or confused, and you might have lots of questions. It's normal to feel this way.

But don't worry! This book is here to help you understand the changes.

We'll talk about why parents might live apart, how it might make you feel, and ways to feel a bit better. Does that sound good?

The most important thing to know is that whatever changes happen in your family, your parents love you and will always be there for you.

Understanding why parents live apart.

When parents aren't happy together and can't live together anymore, they decide to live in separate homes.

Parents might choose this because they argue a lot, can't agree on things, or realize they are happier apart. There can be lots of different reasons.

Your parents won't live in the same home anymore, but they will still care for you. Their love for you has not changed.

We say **separated** or **split up** when parents decide not to live together anymore.

If parents separate when they are married, it's called a **divorce.**

It's not your fault.

Sometimes, when families change, it can make us feel confused. We might start thinking about things we did or didn't do.

But your parents choosing to live apart has nothing to do with you. It's not your fault. This happened because of adult problems between them.

You and your family will all help each other adjust to the changes.

Your parents will always be your parents, and they will always love you and look after you.

New homes and family changes.

When parents split up, they have to think about lots of things, like where you will live.

Each family's situation is different.

You might start living in two homes, one with each parent.

Or, you might live mostly with one parent, or perhaps with grandparents, aunts and uncles or another family, depending on what is going to be best for you.

Families come in all different sizes and shapes. What they all have in common is that they love, protect and care for each other.

New routines.

When your parents are living apart, your daily routine might change as well. Maybe you have a different bedtime routine or different family members picking you up from school.

You might not see each of your parents every day, but maybe you talk to them instead.

It's okay if these changes feel a bit strange or too much at first. Talking to your parents or caregivers about any worries can help.

As time goes on, you might discover new routines that you enjoy. Maybe you'll help make dinner with your dad, or read bedtime stories with your other parent. These new routines can be special, too.

Your questions and worries.

When your parents divorce or decide to live apart, you might have lots of questions in your head and things that worry you.

Ask your grown-ups your questions. They might not have all the answers yet, but talking about how you feel can help.

- Can I still invite friends over to play?
- Will I still get to go to my favorite ice cream shop?
- How often will I see each of you?
- Will you get back together?
- Will I have to change schools?
- What will happen to our hamster?

Remember, your parents love you and want to help you understand what's happening.

- Do you still love me?
- Will you stop fighting?
- Who will take care of me?
- What will we do at Christmas?
- Will I still get to visit my grandparents?
- Can I bring my favorite things with me when I visit?

Understanding your emotions.

Emotions are the way you feel inside. We have lots of different feelings, and our feelings can change from one moment to the next.

Sometimes we even feel two or more feelings at the same time.

It's important to be able to give a name to our feelings and emotions. It helps us understand ourselves better, and it allows us to talk about our feelings with our grown-ups or friends.

When your parents decide not to live together anymore, or get a divorce, you might feel lots of big and different feelings.

worried   nervous   embarrassed   angry

surprised   sad/lonely   relieved   confused

Can you remember times when you've felt any of these feelings?

Your body can give you clues.

Sometimes, your body might also tell you how you're feeling. You might notice your tummy feeling funny or your heart beating faster when you're upset. These signs can help you understand what's going on inside you.

Look at the picture. Can you remember feeling any of these things in your body?

- face feels hot or turns red
- breathing fast
- heart beats fast
- feel sick / not hungry
- making fists
- need the toilet
- shaky legs
- tense muscles
- sweaty hands
- funny feeling in your tummy

Activity: Body Feeling Mapping.

Make your own Body Feeling Map!

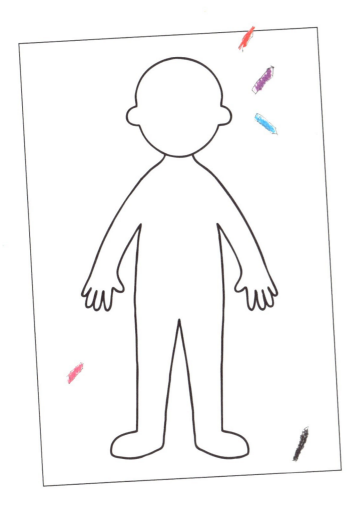

1. On a big sheet of paper, draw the outline of your body.

2. Think about when you feel happy, angry, worried or sad. Choose a color for that feeling.

3. Now, using a colored pencil or crayon. draw some of that color on the place on the body where you feel that emotion.

4. Choose another and another feeling, and repeat. You can also draw pictures or write words.

What do you notice about where you feel things?

Coping strategies.

When you're have big feelings, having strategies or things that help you feel better can make a big difference.

Have you tried doing any of the things in the pictures?

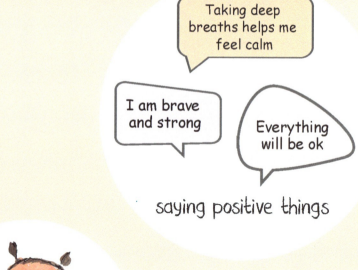
saying positive things

taking a break

doing things you enjoy

mindfulness or deep breathing

doing some exercise

asking for a hug

1, 2, 3...10

counting to 10

Remember, it's ok to have big feelings. You can find lots of ways to help you feel calmer again.

And always know, you're never alone. There are people who care about you and are here to support you.

Your caring circle.

When there are big changes at home, it can be hard, but remember, you're not alone.

Your family can give you love and hugs and make you feel safe.

Friends can play with you and make you smile.

Other adults, like teachers or counsellors, can listen and give you advice.

Whenever you need someone to talk to or just a hug, remember that your family, friends, and other grown-ups who care about you are there for you.

Activity:

1. In the centre of the circle, write your name or draw a picture of your face.

2. Then, write the names of your family, friends and other trusted adults in the other circles.

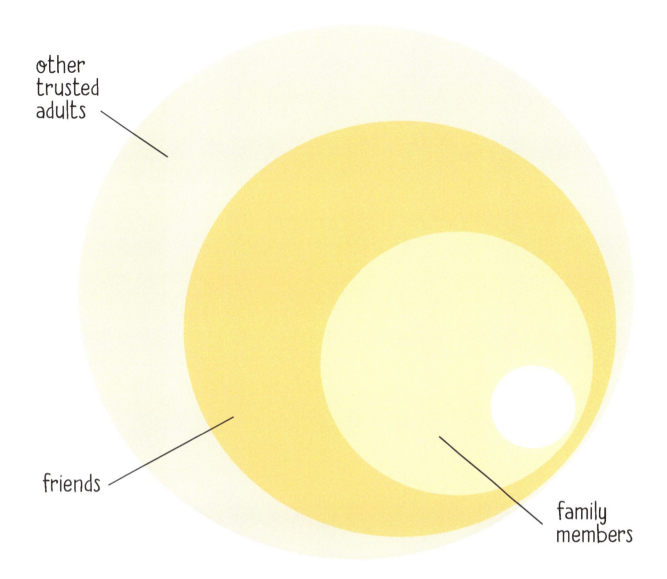

Your feelings and needs.

It's really important to talk about how we're feeling with our families because it helps us take care of each other.

For example, maybe you need some time by yourself. Or perhaps you are finding something difficult. Don't be shy about saying it. Your grown-ups want to know what you are feeling so they can look after you.

> Can I bring my special blanket when I visit papa?

> I need to be quiet now.

> Can we have a family game night? I miss spending time together.

"I'm feeling nervous about tomorrow. Can we talk about it together?"

Don't be afraid to tell grown-ups what you are feeling or ask for what you need.

"Switching houses makes me sad. Can we make it easier?"

"I don't feel like talking right now."

Adults have feelings and needs, just like you do. Sometimes they might need some time alone. Just as you feel good when someone understands your feelings, it's important to understand and respect theirs too.

Expressing your feelings.

Did you know there are lots of ways to show how you feel when you have big emotions, like feeling sad or angry?

Look at the pictures here. Have you tried doing any of these when you have big feelings?

listening to music or dancing

running or doing exercise

When adults argue.

Sometimes, grown-ups might have disagreements or arguments, especially during a divorce. It's important to know that it's not your fault and that it's okay to feel upset or confused when this happens.

Remember, conflicts between adults are between them, and they still love you very much. You can help by staying calm, listening, and not taking sides.

> If you feel scared or uncomfortable, talk to a trusted adult about your feelings. They can help you understand what's happening and make sure you're okay.

Looking after yourself.

It's really important to take care of both your body and your mind. Can you think of any ways you can do this?

Stay active! Doing exercise, like running, jumping, or playing outside, helps our bodies feel strong and happy.

Eat healthy foods: They give you the energy you need to play and learn. They also help your brain work better and make you feel more relaxed.

Take breaks: If you're tired or things are too much, take a break. Find a quiet spot and breathe deeply.

Rest. Make sure you get plenty of sleep each night. After a goodnight's sleep, we are more able to manage things.

Be kind to yourself: Remember, it's okay to make mistakes. Be gentle with yourself, just like you would with a friend.

About change.

Change is like an adventure. It can be exciting, but it can be scary too.

But guess what? You're really brave and strong. Remember when you learned something new, like tying your shoes or riding a bike? It was tricky at first, but with practice, we get better at everything.

Family changes are a bit like that too. At first, they might seem hard, but with time, you'll figure things out and feel more comfortable.

If you're feeling sad because things are different, sharing your feelings with someone you trust can make a huge difference. They might not be able to make everything the same as before, but they can help you feel a bit better.

It's okay if change feels hard right now. With time, things will start to feel better. And never, ever forget how loved you are!

All about you.

My name is _____.

I am ____ years old.

My birthday is _____.

This is me.

draw your picture here!

And this is my home.

draw your home or homes here!

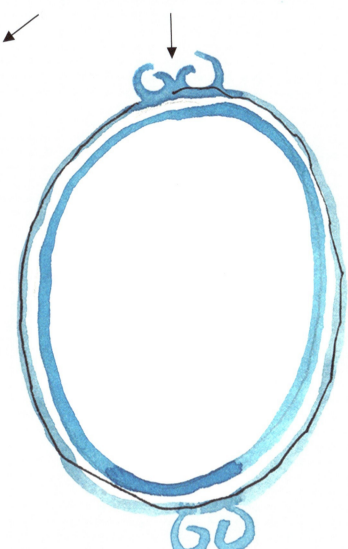

Colour your feelings.

It's natural to have lots of feelings about what's happening in your family. You might feel sad, mad, confused, worried, and even happy sometimes!

Sometimes feelings can be hard to express with words, but art can help us show how we feel inside.

How do you feel since your parents separated? Can you draw it?

My questions.

Think of some questions that you'd like to ask your adult and write them below.

Things we love about...

Write your name in the circle below. Then, ask a few family members to each tell you two or three things they think are great about you, and write them around the circle.

Your 5 senses.

When you're feeling uncomfortable, it can help to pay attention to what's around you.

Find somewhere to sit, relax your body and breathe.

Now find...

5 things you can see

4 things you can feel
(like the ground under your feet, your clothes, a breeze)

3 things you can hear

2 things you can smell

1 thing you can taste

Dear Reader,

Thank you for choosing to read *The Kids' Book of Family Changes* with your child – I hope you both found it helpful.

If you could spare a few minutes to leave me a review online, I'd love to recieve your feedback.

This book forms part of The Kids' Books of Social Emotional Learning series, which also includes:

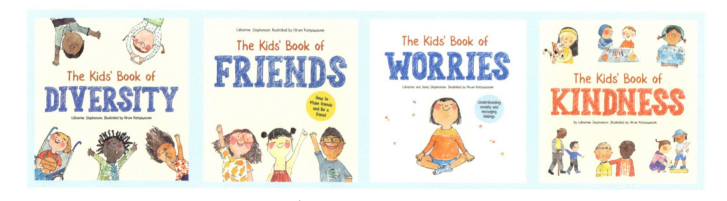

Thank you so much for your support and interest in our books!

Catherine
woodenhousebooks.com

About the author and the illustrator.

Catherine (author)

Catherine is from the UK and spent her childhood in Wales, where she loved roller-skating and Enid Blyton books. She now lives with her partner, son and two cats in Barcelona. She is a freelance translator from Spanish and Catalan into English and a writer. Her own books include social and emotional learning books for children - on friendship, diversity, kindness family changes, worries and emotional regulation - and dual language (Spanish-English) stories.

Hiruni (illustrator)

Hiruni is from Sri Lanka and lives in her hometown, Ambalangoda. She holds a Bachelor's Degree in Fashion Design from the University of Moratuwa, and today is a full-time illustrator. She enjoys doing paintings, fine illustrations, and especially illustrations for children's books in her unique style, mixing digital and watercolour techniques. She also loves fashion, nature and reading.

You can find us at:

WOODEN HOUSE BOOKS

woodenhousebooks.com
IG @woodenhousebooks

www.ingramcontent.com/pod-product-compliance
Ingram Content Group UK Ltd.
Pitfield, Milton Keynes, MK11 3LW, UK
UKHW051426190325
5066UKWH00019B/139